The Definitive Darts Coaching Manual

Your pathway to success

by

David Kirby

The Definitive Darts Coaching Manual

ISBN: 978-1-907540-54-7

Published January 2012
Reprinted 2nd Edition April 2012

Printed and Published by Anchorprint Group Limited
www.anchorprint.co.uk

Preface

Why have you picked this coaching manual up? Perhaps you are interested in:

➤ Personal development

➤ Working as a coach

➤ Pure interest

The primary reason for this manual is to assist with coaching the darts player. It is an in-depth study concentrating on the physiology and psychology involved in being the best darts player you could be.

For my part I have been involved for many years in coaching athletics and martial arts. I have endeavoured to bring the discipline used within these sports in to the darts arena.

Over the last few seasons I have played in and latterly managed a successful county darts Super League team.

The following pages are a coaching guide aimed at a majority of players. We all know players who have phenomenal flare and unbridled talent. Some have extremely strange styles. Some spend time at the oche chastising themselves after every throw. Some celebrate wildly after hitting a 180 or a great out shot. Others wind up the opposition and the crowd plus get involved in gamesmanship… these I would suggest are the few and as mentioned at the start of this paragraph, this manual is aimed at the majority and not the minority.

The aim of the following chapters is to develop the ability to keep a high level of concentration, focus during games, keep your pulse rate under control and to have a mantra and routine that works for you and your game.

There will also be sections on practice routines. These will be split into three:

➤ Enhance your game at whatever standard (DR1)

➤ Professional routine (DR2)

➤ Step change/bespoke (DR3)

The above routines will be explained in detail and they should form the backbone of your future darting experience.

Introduction

The following items will be discussed in detail throughout this manual. Areas of significant note will be marked in the text as a **key point**.

There will also be space for you to write notes, as this whole book is designed to assist with coaching and it may be beneficial to jot down some of your own notes and observations

I suggest a first read through this manual, perhaps highlighting some areas to focus on again when reading in more detail.

Warm Up Phase

It is important to create a routine in the warm up phase that works for you.

You will have to consider factors like:

➢ Fatigue

➢ Starting times

➢ Facilities

➢ Time allowed at the board

Key Point: *You will need to warm up both mind and body.*

Some players are known for extremely long warm up sessions whilst others may hit the board after only a few throws. As I said at the start of this chapter we need to create a routine that works for you but that is flexible enough to cope with the differing conditions you may face.

I would like us to consider four warm up phases:

➢ Pre arrival at the venue

➢ Warm up phase at the venue

➢ Pre match warm up

➢ Pre practice/training warm up

Starting with the *Pre arrival at the venue.* All the sessions should start with a relaxed throw and a general area as a target. The concentration and conditioning still plays a part, even in this warm up. Here you concentrate on being relaxed, throwing a straight dart and aiming within a general area of the board.

Ten to fifteen minutes should suffice. You can work with this and develop a time that suits you. You may also wish to divide the general aiming segments in to areas of the board. For instance, 5 minutes and a segment (three numbers) at the top, 5 minutes at a segment on the left and so on.

This whole phase is designed to warm your mind up and leave the brain aware of what is required and what is to come. So the next part after the general darts is to focus on doubles. You will only need about 15 minutes.

The doubles chosen should include the **Infamous 10** plus a dozen or so you wish to practise. Once you have developed the 20 or so you wish to practise write them down. Then print them off and stick the list up near your practice board.

This list becomes the selection of doubles that will be used to warm your mind up.

Key Point: *If after two darts you have left your finish with an odd number. Concentrate on your last dart to leave the score as sensible as possible. No wasted darts. This is all part of the conditioning and will prevent you from throwing wasted darts during a game.*

Pre Match Warm Up:

Now that your arm and mind are warm you can consider this phase before your match starts. Every one will be slightly different here but you won't go far wrong if you plan to have an hour throwing at this stage.

We have seen that we have tuned our mind to doubles and the arm is relaxed and throwing straight and consistent darts. So what to do for the next hour.

You may find that if there is a group of you at the venue a few games of singles and or pairs may suffice. Some may like to have a group finishing competition working up the doubles.

If you look around the room, you may notice the more successful players will be concentrating on their own pre match warm up over this next 60 minutes.

So how do we structure this session? We must ensure that what ever we choose is not stressful but prepares us for that moment when we are called to oche for the start of our first game. If you have a routine that already works for you then stay with it. You may wish to experiment with a few others, so we will explore a couple of examples.

Switch:
The aim is to hit 100 within the three darts. If you achieve this, then immediately switch next throw to a 32 score left. The idea is to check this out without busting it. If you hit the 32 1st or 2nd dart then the go is over. Now switch back to the 20s and so on. After 20 minutes change the double to 40 and for the last 20 minutes use 36. If you do not achieve either the 100 or the 32, then stay with it until you do and then go for the switch.

170 Game:
This game sees you playing an imaginary opponent. You start with a score of 170 and you have 9 nine darts to check it out with. If you succeed you take a point. If you fail then you remove a point. It would be useful to have a positive score at the end of this

session. This game helps on many fronts, mental arithmetic, and concentration and is mildly competitive.

Fatigue factor

Prior to starting the game you must make sure you still have the energy and stamina to maintain a high standard of concentration and focus.

A 2-hour evening tournament may see you at the oche for a least an hour and a half. This may equate to throwing competitive darts for a total of 45 minutes. It may not seem a lot when you read it on paper. But you need to remember that this is high intensity, focused and full-on concentration.

We have discussed the warm up stage and the pre match warm up. In total we could have 1 and 1/4 hours at the practice boards and 45 minutes competitive throwing. So in total that would be at least two hours at the oche.

To allow us to achieve the consistent standard during the game, it is important that we have developed our full practice routine to include a stamina session during the week. Without this we cannot prepare our bodies to cope adequately with the rigours of the competitive game.

Finally you may have a question of how long to have between the end of the pre match warm up phase and the actual game. Again you may already have an idea of what works for you. You may not have really thought of it yet.

To get this right a little planning is involved. Firstly you need to have rough idea of when your game starts. Then work back 60 minutes and this will be the start of your pre match warm up. I would suggest you aim to take as short a break as possible before you start the actual match. Over time you can experiment with this and develop the exact period that works best for you.

So in summary let us imagine you approaching an evening three match session with multiple boards and constant games starting at 8pm:

> ➤ 5.00 pm at home 15 minutes on the **infamous 10 plus your extra doubles (just go through these straight through. Do not keep going until you hit one. This warm up is more about tuning your mind).**

> ➤ 6.45 pm arrive at venue

> ➢ 6.45 pm start 15 minutes general warm up
> ➢ 7.00 pm start 60 minutes pre match warm up
> ➢ 8.00 pm commence game(s)

Note, as long as the break is not over 5 minutes between matches, a warm up at the oche at the start of the next game should suffice. If longer then revert back to a considered practice session to keep warm.

Temperament and the Game

Composure: Except for the few, the approach should be to maintain a steady focused rhythm whilst keeping the pulse rate under control.

This is often seen in similar disciplines, like archery and target rifle shooting. The shooter will spend a considerable amount of time before approaching their shoot acclimatising to the light and lowering their heart rate. Imagine looking through the sights of a rifle at a target 25 metres away, hitting a bull and then jumping up and running around before taking the next shot.

You can predict the result! How, though is this any different to hitting a maximum 180 at darts? When John Lowe hit his TV 9 darter, he kept his composure through all nine darts. The same applies for the rifle shooter. If they have a poor shot, do they swear and curse stomping to the board? No, they re- focus, gain composure and continue with their shot.

As mentioned at the beginning, some players, a few well known ones can and do thrive on the showmanship element on the oche. They can hit 180, turn and gesture to the crowd and still find the composure to continue and hit big scores! This may be to "gee" themselves up or perhaps to play to an audience. The majority of players should adopt the approach used within the rifle range.

Key Point: Be Mr/Mrs Cool. Eliminate from now any signs of emotion. Keep the heart rate under control. Approach the throw in a controlled and consistent manner. Do not swear.

This is though always your choice. To see the negative side of what I have explained above. Watch the player who cannot control their emotions. The throw will be inconsistent and the harder they try, more often the throw becomes worse. This may have been you. If you are serious about improving your darts, then really think about the next time your step up to the oche.

Key Point: It may help to develop a mantra. By this I mean when you practise at home you have a saying/picture/theme in your mind as you focus on the game. This is used for instance in golf and snooker when approaching a match winning put or shot.

You may have created an image of you throwing like Phil Taylor. Steady, accurate and controlled. In practice you aim well, release in a piston like fashion and stay focused on the target. Good, so when you step up in the game, perhaps in your mind each time you repeat, throw like Phil Taylor. No one else needs to know. Over time your mind will adopt your training routine and overlay it during the live game using the mantra as a trigger point.

Tournaments: You arrive at a competition and there are 128 entered. You look around and the room seems crowded. Well if this is a knock out tournament there will only be 7 you need to beat to win the whole competition.

Warm Up: Whether playing in a world tournament or a local pub match, your approach should be planned and consistent.

Do not rush the warm up and you control the oche. If you are only allowed 9 darts, then use them all and use them well.

If the scorer has not arrived or they are allowing as many practice darts as you wish, then pop back into one of your comfortable practice routines. Let some one else worry about when it should start.

Key Point: *Keep the pulse rate under control.*

If the scorer still has not arrived, allow your opponent to worry about this. Let them go to the desk to talk with the officials; you just keep on with your practice routine.

The Game: Are you a watcher or do you look away. No problem which. Firstly if you are watcher, then decide now if the opponent scoring well intimidates you or inspires you.

Be very honest with this assessment and think back through all your recent matches.

The constant thud of treble 20 before your eyes. What are you actually thinking and how are you reacting? If you can watch with no adverse effect and if this perhaps even inspires you, they stay with it.

Alternatively you may need to develop a routine that allows you to remain focussed on the game whilst not suffering by watching your opponents' darts.

Some players if allowed will nip back to take a drink between throws. Others will stand back and look away. Take time to develop a routine that you feel comfortable with.

If you are now focussed on you and not them, it will be advisable to glance at the scoreboard before your throw. This will tell you what they have scored, what they have left and importantly what you have left.

The scoreboard in front of you may now change your approach for your next scoring sequence. For instance they have hit 140 leaving 32. You are sitting on 90. As explained in the finishing section, T18 is NOT the shot, as a single 18 will leave you 72, and without hitting a Bull/treble/single there is no two dart out shot unless you go double double. So treble 20 is the best option. If you miss the treble, then one more 20 leaves you a bull to win the leg.

There is a saying:

> *"Look at what you are aiming at and aim at what you are looking at"*

What does this mean to you? When you approach the dartboard with three darts, we have agreed your focus and concentration levels must be high. Thus allowing you the optimal chance of a high success rate at your chosen target.

A loss of concentration and DRIFT occurs and at least one of the darts will not hit the intended target.

Key Point: *During the practice sessions it is important that you develop this high level of concentration.*

To do this we have talked about a mantra. ("I am Phil Taylor" for example). You must employ this before you throw each and every dart, whether in a game or in a practice routine.

We are aiming to achieve conditioning by being relaxed, focused and repetitive.

So perhaps a mantra could be RFR… Relaxed/Focused/Repetitive

This last key point is extremely important. We must maximise both our time at the board practising and during a game.

During the practice phase imagine just throwing three darts at the general area of the treble 20 without much thought behind it. Imagine doing this for an hour or so. You may say you have had an hour at the board. Though just think about it, the damage done. You have conditioned your body in this session to throw loose darts with limited purpose and probably done it quite well.

It would have been better to spend 10 minutes totally focused, using your mantra, than the wasted hour.

Finishing

An interesting area in the whole aspect of playing darts. As you progress through this chapter, you will develop an understanding of the nuances and fundamentals of finishing a game of darts.

We have all heard that well-worn cliché: *trebles for show and doubles for dough.* Well if you don't finish the game first…you lose.

Areas we will look at:

> ➢ When to start thinking of a double finish
> ➢ Do you have 1, 2 or 3 darts in your hand?
> ➢ What is your opponent on?
> ➢ Your preferred route
> ➢ Are you playing single or pairs?
> ➢ Who has the darts?
> ➢ Is the bull an option?
> ➢ Can you pressure?
> ➢ All the combinations
> ➢ Practice routines

Once you have mastered this aspect, you will start to notice possible opportunities in the games that you are playing.

Even at Super League level you may see your opponent sitting on 128 for instance and you are on 32. They step up to the oche and the first dart slams into the big 20….. Time to get your darts ready. They now have no two-dart finish as they are now on 108. The throw should have been, perhaps a big or treble 18. Thus leaving them either 74 or 110. (60 & bull).

So the game has started and we are into the leg, when to start thinking of the finish.? Well you may argue that it could depend on your darting ability or your mathematical confidence.

Key Point: *From now on we will focus on you having the ability to take on the big finishes and that by the time you have worked through this manual and practised, your darts' maths brain will also be vastly improved.*

I think we all agree that 170 is the highest finish available to us. Also 180 is the highest score we can hit with three darts. Therefore in this manual we will start reviewing our finishing options from 350 onwards.

But before we get in to the detail of working through all the combinations, it is imperative to focus on the collection of finishes that are fundamental to the game.

I am talking about the area between 90 and 135. So often you see great scoring players come undone by not learning and practising the following combinations.

You may find it helpful to work through the full list of finishes in slow time and maybe jot down some observations and your own preferences.

For now though you must embrace this next section.

As we go through these finishing combinations, treble 20 is often the default first dart.

We will mention it but the detail and explanation will be around the more specific areas.

If you take nothing else from this manual, at least learn the following:

Key Point: *The Infamous 10 finishes:*

90	20-20-Bull 60-D15 20-60-D5	If your opponent is on a finish, you must consider this option. Missing the treble 18 does not leave a two dart out shot without you having to hit a double or treble on your next dart.
119	57-leaving 62 19-leaving 100	If you went 20s and hit a single you would be left on 99. This then does not leave you a two dart out shot.
122	54-leaving 68 18-leaving 104	If you went 20s and hit a single you would be left on 102. This then does not leave you a two dart out shot.
123	57-leaving 66 19- leaving 104	If you went 20s and hit a single you would be left on 103. This then does not leave you a two dart out shot.

125	Bull-leaving 75 25-leaving 100 54-leaving 71	If you went 20s and hit a single you would be left on 105. This then does not leave you a two dart out shot.
126	57-leaving 69 19-leaving 107	If you went 20s and hit a single you would be left on 106. This then does not leave you a two dart out shot.
128	54-leaving 74 18-leaving 110	If you went 20s and hit a single you would be left on 108. This then does not leave you a two dart out shot.
129	57-leaving 72 19 leaving 110	If you went 20s and hit a single you would be left on 109. This then does not leave you a two dart out shot.
132	Bull-leaving 82 25-leaving 107	If you went 20s and hit a single you would be left on 112. This then does not leave you a two dart out shot.
135	Bull-leaving 85 25-leaving 110	If you went 20s and hit a single you would be left on 115. This then does not leave you a two dart out shot.

Hopefully as you glance through this **Infamous 10** you will see the benefit of not initially going for a treble 20. You may have slightly different initial shots that you have practised and worked through. There is space in the margins to note down some alternatives.

From now on you will be able to eradicate these finishing errors from your game. Also your opponent may judge you slightly differently, perhaps with a little more respect. It is to note that in some games the margin between winning and losing may be that slight.

Now as we come to review all the finishes it is important to be aware of a few factors. If you are really serious about improving your game, you will need to sit down and review your approach and learn all the options along with aggravating factors. By this I mean:

➢ Where is the opponent in the game

➢ Your preferred route

➢ Percentage numbers (see below)

➢ Your ability

An example could be: Your opponent is on 32 and you are on 41 and this is the deciding leg in the match. You have the darts.

You know if you miss your opponent has 3 darts to win on a fairly comfortable double.

You may be on fire and single 9 is the shot for you, leaving you 2 darts to win going for 32.

Key Point: *This is where you need to sit and review options that can be available to you in this situation and think them through and then practice them.*

You may come up with the conclusion that in this situation a guaranteed shot at a double is the preferred option. Therefore perhaps a dart at the wire between small 3 and small 17. This leaving either 38 or 24 for your finish. This could be better in this tight finish than perhaps missing the 9 and having to rectify the position before one dart to win the match.

As I said earlier this is your choice. You must have worked all these scenarios out at the practice board, so when it arises during the match, single 17 double 12 and you win.

It is also worth remembering, it can be a risk going for a single number to leave a finish where the treble of that number can bust you. I.e. 56 left and you go for big 20 to leave 36…risky. May be better to opt for the 16 thus leaving tops. And no chance of busting the score.

Further Finishes:

These are purely for discussion; it is up to you to decide your preferences. There will be many other options, which you know or you have seen players throw. Remember to record them and have a think about the merits and where and when you might use them.

If the two darts option changes the choice, we will mention it for discussion. (These two darts options will be shown in brackets.)

Where there are multiple options, I have listed them in what I consider to be the optimal order.

41	9-leaving 32 or 17 or 3 Leaving 24 or 38	As mentioned above, the way out depends at what stage of the game you are at and how you feel.
42	10-leaving 32 6-leaving 36	10 & 6 next door so perfect choice.
43	3-leaving 40	Seems sensible especially as there are odd numbers either side of the 3.
44	4-leaving 40 12-leaving 32 8-leaving 36 16-leaving 28	4 would seem the best option as 18 covers the loose throw.
45	5-leaving 40 13-leaving 32	Personal choice
46	10-leaving 36 6-leaving 40	10 & 6 next door so perfect choice.
47	7-leaving 40 15-leaving 32 19-leaving 28	7 has more protection with 19 as cover.

48	16-leaving 32 8-leaving 40	No sensible other way.
49	9-leaving 40 17-leaving 32 13-leaving 36	The 17 route does have the possibility of a bust score if you hit 51.
50	10-leaving 40 18-leaving 32	10 the best route to avoid a bust score.
51	11-leaving 40 19-leaving 32	Again watch the bust if you go for 19s.
52	12-leaving 40 20-leaving 32	Watch the bust if you go for 20s
53	13-leaving 40 17-leaving 36	The best option.
54	14-leaving 40 18-leaving 36	Watch the bust if you go for 18s.
55	15-leaving 40	The best option.
56	16-leaving 40 20-leaving 36	Watch the bust if you go for 20s
57	17-leaving 40	The best option.
58	18-leaving 40	The best option.
59	19-leaving 40	The best option.
60	20-leaving 40 (30-leaving 30)	Aim high to avoid busting your score. (Going treble 10, a single 10 at least leaves Bull).
61	45-leaving 16 25-leaving 36 (33-leaving 28)	A lot of people go the 25 route, but a bull will leave you 11, which is a little tricky under pressure. (A single 11 leaves Bull).
62	30-leaving 32 (36-leaving 26)	Treble 10 is the option but double 15 is not a problem. (A single 12 leaves Bull).
63	51-leaving 12 (39-leaving 24)	Best option a single 17 leaves 46, which is ok to split when under pressure. (A single 13 leaves Bull).

64	48-leaving 16 24-leaving 40 (14-leaving Bull)	Pleasant area to throw at, treble 16 and treble 8. (With the 14 an accurate shot at the inside of the double 14 is interesting as the double would leave 36 and the single would leave the Bull).
65	25-leaving 40 33-leaving 32 (45-leaving 20)	Personal choice as a single 11 still leaves 54. (A single 15 leaves Bull).
66	30-leaving 36 (48-leaving 18)	The best choice with three darts. With 2 darts left go treble 16 double 9. (A single 16 still leaves the Bull).
67	51-leaving 16	The best shot. (A single 17 leaves Bull).
68	60-leaving 8 (54-leaving 14)	20s the best route. (A single 18 leaves Bull).
69	57-leaving 12 45-leaving 24	The best shot. (A single 19 leaves Bull).
70	30-leaving 40 54-leaving 16 38-leaving 32 (60-leaving 10)	All have good back up scenarios if you miss the treble. You decide based upon your preferred finish. (A single 20 leaves Bull).
71	39-leaving 32 51-leaving 20	The best option. A single 13 leaves 58.
72	32-leaving 40 36-leaving 36 48-leaving 24 60-leaving 12	All have good back up scenarios if you miss the treble. You decide based upon your preferred finish.
73	57-leaving 16 33-leaving 40	The 19s are the best option leaving 54 if you hit a single,
74	42-leaving 32 54-leaving 20	A single 14 leaves 60.
75	51-leaving 24 45-leaving 30 (25-leaving Bull)	A single 17 leaves 18 then tops. A single 15 leaves 20 then tops. You choose.
76	60-leaving 16	The best option. A single 20 leaves 56.

77	57-leaving 20	The best option. A single 19 leaves 58.
78	54-leaving 24	The best option. A single 18 leaves 60.
79	57-leaving 22 51-leaving 28	With three darts in your hand you may prefer the 19s route, Also worth think about partners if playing pairs.
80	60-leaving 20 54-leaving 26 48-leaving 32 (60-leaving 20) (tops tops)	Three main options here. Quite a lot of personal choice involved. Depends if you miss the treble on the second two combinations you will be likely going for a bull for your out shot.
81	57-leaving 24 45-leaving 36	The best option. A single 19 leaves 62.
82	Bull-leaving 32 42-leaving 40	Going for the bull if a 25 is hit then at least you have a 17 leaving tops.
83	51-leaving 32	The best option. A single 17 leaves 66.
84	60-leaving 24	The best option. A single 20 leaves 64..... Note 14 only for bull; do not be tempted to throw at treble 16 if you only have two darts in your hand. A single 16 or single 8 do not leave you a shot out.
85	45-leaving 40	The best option. A single 15 leaves 70.
86	54-leaving 32 60-leaving 26	The 54 option is lovely as a single 18 leaves you another 18 for a shot at the bull.
87	51-leaving 36	The best option. A single 17 leaves 70.
88	60-leaving 28	The best option. A single 20 leaves 68.

89	57-leaving 32	The best option. A single 19 leaves 70.
90	54-leaving 36 Bull-leaving 40 20-20-Bull 60-leaving 30 20-60-D5	If your opponent is on a finish, you must consider the 20s option. Missing the treble 18 does not leave a two out shot without you having to hit a double or treble on your next dart.
91	51-leaving 40 Bull/25-leaving 41/66	Personal choice.
92	60-leaving 32 Bull/25-leaving 42/67	Personal choice.
93	57-leaving 36 Bull/25-leaving 43/68	Personal choice.
94	54-leaving 40 Bull/25-leaving 44/69	Personal choice.
95	57-leaving 38	The only option if you have two darts in your hand.
96	60-leaving 36	The best option.
97	57-leaving 40	The best option.
98	60-leaving 38	You may wish to amend this depending on your opponent's score.
99	Do what you want!	No two dart finish. Perhaps start with 57 to leave 42 or 60 to leave 39.
100	60-leaving 40	The best option.
101	60-leaving 41 (51-leaving bull)	If you have three darts in your hand, the problem with going for the 51 first is if you hit a 2 you now do not have a 2 dart out shot.

102	60-leaving 42 48-leaving 54	An interesting one, as here with the 48 there are a huge range of good misses available still leaving you a finish. Just a thought.
103	60-leaving 43 57-leaving 46	Back to personal choice.
104	54-leaving 50 60-leaving 44 57-leaving 47	Two darts and you have to go for the 18s. The problem with the 20s is a single 5 leaves you 99 and no two dart out shot.
105	60-leaving 45	The best option.
106	60-leaving 46	The best option.
107	57-leaving 50	Two darts and you have to go for the 19s and it is probable the best choice with three darts as well.
108	54-leaving 54 60-leaving 48 57-leaving 51	Back to personal choice. A single 18 though does leave you a shot at treble 18 for a 36 out shot.
109	60-leaving 49 57-leaving 52	Personal choice. Both have good second dart options.
110	60-leaving 50	The best option.
111	60-leaving 51 51-leaving 60	Personal choice. Both have good second dart options.
112	60-leaving 52	The best option.
113	60-leaving 53	The best option.
114	60-leaving 54	The best option.
115	60-leaving 55	The best option.
116	60-leaving 56	The best option.
117	60-leaving 57 57-leaving 60	Personal choice. Both have good second dart options.
118	60-leaving 58 54-leaving 64	Personal choice. Both have good second dart options.

119	57-leaving 62 19-leaving 100	If you went 20s and hit a single you would be left on 99. This then does not leave you a two dart out shot.
120	60-leaving 60	The best option.
121	60-leaving 61 51-leaving 70	Personal choice. Both have good second dart options.
122	54-leaving 68 18-leaving 104	If you went 20s and hit a single you would be left on 102. This then does not leave you a two dart out shot.
123	57-leaving 66 19- leaving 104	If you went 20s and hit a single you would be left on 103. This then does not leave you a two dart out shot.
124	60-leaving 64	The best option.
125	Bull-leaving 75 25-leaving 100	If you went 20s and hit a single you would be left on 105. This then does not leave you a two dart out shot.
126	57-leaving 69 19-leaving 107	If you went 20s and hit a single you would be left on 106. This then does not leave you a two dart out shot.
127	60-leaving 67	The best option.
128	54-leaving 74 18-leaving 110	If you went 20s and hit a single you would be left on 108. This then does not leave you a two dart out shot.
129	57-leaving 72 19 leaving 110	If you went 20s and hit a single you would be left on 109. This then does not leave you a two dart out shot.
130	60-leaving 70	The best option.
131	60-leaving 71	The best option.
132	Bull-leaving 82 25-leaving 107	If you went 20s and hit a single you would be left on 112.

		This then does not leave you a two dart out shot.
133	60-leaving 73	The best option.
134	60-leaving 74	The best option.
135	Bull-leaving 85 25-leaving 110	If you went 20s and hit a single you would be left on 115. This then does not leave you a two dart out shot .
136	60-leaving 76	The best option.
137	60-leaving 77	The best option.
138	60-leaving 78	The best option.
139	60-leaving 79	The best option.
140	60-leaving 80 54-leaving 86	The second option has merit.
141	60-leaving 81	The best option.
142	60-leaving 82	The best option.
143	60-leaving 83	The best option.
144	60-leaving 84 54-leaving 90	Personal choice.
145	60-leaving 85	The best option.
146	60-leaving 86	The best option.
147	60-leaving 87	The best option.
148	60-leaving 88	The best option.
149	60-leaving 89	The best option.
150	60-leaving 90 57-leaving 93	An interesting second option.
151	60-leaving 91	The best option.
152	60-leaving 92	The best option.
153	60-leaving 93	The best option.

154	60-leaving 94	The best option.
155	60-leaving 95	The best option.
156	60-leaving 96	The best option.
157	60-leaving 97	The best option.
158	60-leaving 98	The best option.
159	XXX	What are you doing here on this score? No three dart finish!!
160	60-leaving 100	The best option.
161	60-leaving 101	The best option.
162	XXX	What are you doing here on this score? No three dart finish!!
163	XXX	What are you doing here on this score? No three dart finish!!
164	60-leaving 104	The best option.
165	XXX	What are you doing here on this score? No three dart finish!!
166	XXX	What are you doing here on this score? No three dart finish!!
167	60-leaving 107	The best option.
168	XXX	What are you doing here on this score? No three dart finish!!
169	XXX	What are you doing here on this score? No three dart finish!!
170	60-leaving 110	The best option. And what a lovely way to finish.

Advanced ideas:

As you become more comfortable with your maths and finishes, you will need to just think about score a little ahead of 170. By this I mean, imagine being on 229. Scoring 20, 20 and 20 would leave you the bogey 169. Here with your last dart, a 19 would have been a better shot.

This is not always easy to work out in the heat of a match or indeed during the throw.

Firstly you should get into the practice of subtracting 170 from your score whilst your opponent is throwing. This will give you an indication of the minimum score required to give you a three dart out shot at the next visit to the board. Once you have acquired this skill, you will be able to refine the maths to make sure you don't leave 159, 162, 163, 165, 166, 168 and 169.

As a fall back to above system, you will also note that below and including 158 there is always a three dart finish. Therefore it is quite a good idea if the exact maths is not with you; just make sure the scoring darts take you below 159.

For example you are on 258. Using the first method you take 170 off and you see you need 88 to leave the first finish. And with the second method a straight 100 leave you in the clear street. So straight away a 100 score at least is your target

Percentage of 40/32/36:

Looking at the preferred finishes from above. If you take 40 through to 100. The finishes 40, 36 and 32 equate to 73% of the preferred outs. In detail:

➢ 40 = 36%

➢ 36 = 14%

➢ 32 = 23%

The percentage may change slightly as you progress through to 170 but already you can see where your focus should be. We will discuss practice routines later in this chapter.

From the above table three quarters of your out shots will come from three numbers.

During the switch routines that we discuss later in the book, these three should make up the main three sessions.

Practice routines for finishes:

I have split practice routines into three categories:

> ➤ General practice
> ➤ Conditioning
> ➤ Mind warm up.

General Practice: Wherever you look there are many games played to allow you to go around the board throwing at doubles.

A good start would be the **Bob Anderson 29**: Each player begins with 29 points to his name; the game is played on one board with each player taking three darts in rotation.

The first three darts are all thrown at double 1, every double 1 scored is added to that players score, should the player miss double 1 the value of that double is subtracted from the 29 points, i.e. player scores 2 double ones, score is added to the 29 making 33, player misses with all three darts at double one, the value of the double; 2 is deducted from the 29 points = 27.

After all players competing have thrown at double one the procedure is repeated on double 2, double 3 and so on with the game ending on the centre bull, should any player miss doubles and run out of points i.e. player is on double 6 but only has 11 points to his credit, misses double 6 value of 12 he does not have enough points to continue (11- 12 leaves −1), that player is then eliminated from the game and will mark for the other players for the duration of the match.

The player who has the most points after the last double is thrown at; 50-centre bull, wins the match.

As a guide to scoring, if you can reach 100 points before double 9 you should post a good overall total, John Lowe has been in the 300s consistently, over 400 quite a few times and has recorded a top score of 747.

Twenty-nine is a great way to practise on those all important doubles but much more than that it makes the player use the whole circumference of the board, every eye contact versus number location that is possible to make. You can play it on your own and record your total score.

It may be you choose to build this in to your weekly session and over a period of time you can analyse the results.

Conditioning will be achieved by using the Switch Routines as described in the Practice Chapter.

Basically this session is designed to increase your focus and concentration. You start with 20s. The aim is to hit 100 within the three darts. If you achieve this, them immediately switch next throw to a 32 score left. The idea is to check this out without busting it. If you hit the 32 1st or 2nd dart then the go is over. Now switch back to the 20s and so on. If you do not achieve either the 100 or the 32, stay with it until you do, then go for the switch.

Record how many Switches you hit in this session. Keep this figure as part of your training record. Note one switch is hitting the 100 and then the double or visa versa.

As we have seen previous in this chapter, 40, 32 and 36 make up 73% of the out shots from 40 to 100. So, the switch routine can be split into three sessions focussing on these numbers.

Mind Warm Up: This whole phase is designed to warm your mind up and leave the brain aware of what is required and what is to come. You will only need about 15 minutes. This is a session designed to use prior to a game.

The doubles chosen should include the **Infamous 10** plus a dozen of so you wish to practise. Once you have developed the 20 or so you wish to practise write them down. Then print them off and stick the list up near your practice board.

Equipment

In this chapter we will look at all aspects from clothing through to your darts.

We will break it down in to the following areas:

- Dart barrels
- Stems
- Flights
- Points
- Dart accessories
- Shirt/blouse and trousers
- Shoes

Note: Only change your dart or accessories as a last resort. If you decide to then the following observations will assist.

I think we all agree that being able to throw a consistent accurate dart is about many factors but here we will concentrate on being able to feel the darts. You will be able to have confidence in all the conditioning you have undertaken and also be able to sense that dart in your fingers and be able to influence the throw.

You may be lucky to be still throwing your original darts from when you first started. Although other factors may now influence the required dart:

- Change in body shape
- Injury
- Updated technique
- Advances in dart manufacture
- Drop off in form
- Personal choice

The factors above may influence you in deciding to change your dart or part of the assembly. So we will start with this area and talk later about clothing and accessories.

Is it a problem if we change our dart? A really interesting debating point. If you are top of the county listings, averaging 30 plus and the number one player to avoid it may seem not the right time to tinker with the equipment.

We mentioned above a few factors that may precipitate looking to change.

With any of the above factors it is not a problem to sit down and reanalyse our throw and what sort of dart we require. We may have started with 27g in our teens and now in our thirties we just feel a lighter dart will help with fatigue and tighter accuracy. Ok, so structure your approach and set up a project plan to make the change work for you.

Step 1: Confirm with yourself and or your coach that a change is required.

Step 2: What is the real issue that requires you to change your dart?

Step 3: Can a change be achieved without a new dart? For example, a new place to throw from on the oche because perhaps your eyesight has deteriorated.

Step 4: Create time to evaluate fully the range of equipment

Step 5: Obtain a selection of flights of all shapes, stems of various lengths and borrow some barrels. With the barrels you will be looking to have weights up and down from yours. Different lengths and different shapes.

Step 6: Now you need to need to get some paper and record a practice session that includes a systematic evaluation whilst maintaining a record or incremental changes. By this I mean don't just throw a new dart, with new shape flights and different length barrels.

Step 7: Hopefully you will have an idea of what you believe the issue to be before you start. So if you have agreed the darts seems to be a little off centre and may be a little quick through the air, you may wish to start with changing your flights. So make this session work for you, you need at least 20 minutes with each set up. Firstly make sure you are fully warmed up using your original darts. Then decide what you will use as a practice session to record your throw. Perhaps for this would be 100s. This is throwing 100 darts at twenties and recording the amount hit. For example you hit 81 (treble 20, single 20 and single 1) that would be 4 twenties. Carry out this first twenty minutes again using your original darts. This allows us to have **control sample** of your current ability.

Next change the piece of equipment, in this case the flights and go again with the next twenties minutes at the 100s. After this you will have some thing like this written down:

> **My dart with pear flight = 96 twenties**
> **My dart with normal flight = 110 twenties**
> **My dart with kite flights = 88 twenties**

This whole process can be carried on with all aspects of the dart. It is though important to remind you that if you change two pieces to start with, you will not be sure of which piece is making the difference.

As you build through this process, the uplift from changing one piece might not be all that you require. Now you can factor in a second change. In the example above it looks like we seem to work better with the normal flights but we would like to be around the 125 score on the twenties practice routine. Now try to factor in using your barrels, normal flights but work again through three sessions using different length stems and record the results.

This incremental process will help you evaluate what actually works best for you. At the start you may agree that the dart, especially the barrel is not working for you. So start perhaps with a new dart and throw a **control sample** for 20 minutes. Again use the manufacturers set up and work through all the combinations to review if the changes have worked for you.

Step 8: Once you have agreed the new set-up, time to get them working for you. To start with you must calibrate them to you. By this I mean for many years you have conditioned yourself to a certain dart configuration and now you have changed it. Your body and throw needs to get used to it.

The longer you have at this juncture the better, especially before your first competitive game.

Key Point: The mental side of your game is now important. After changing your darts, any loss of form or a bad shot has to be either accepted as the bedding in period for the darts, or even that the dart change has not contributed to this. It would extremely counter productive to revert back to your old set-up without a full consolidation period of at least 6 months using this new configuration.

Clothing: A lot has written about footwear and if would seem sensible to have one pair of shoes that you both play and practise in.

Shirts/Blouses and trousers. To some players it may make absolutely no difference on how they feel by what they are dressed in. Other may relish a shirt with their name and club colours on and feels it enhancing their game.

This is a very personal opinion, but if you have not already tried a good quality sports dart shirt, treat yourself, you never know what the uplift may be.

Goal Setting

There is a huge amount written now in sport about the importance of goal setting.

I would recommend working with a limited set, as low as just one or two.

Progress in darts is probably best measured in yearly cycles. It would make sense then to have these annual goals set as building blocks towards an ultimate aim.

The ultimate aim when achieved if worked correctly would have become a new building block to a new target as you continue to progress.

An example could be that your ultimate aim is to play for the county. At present you are a good local league player and see playing Super League now far away. After analysing your game you realise your scoring is not quite at the required level.

So back to Goal Setting. This season your local league has a competition for the most 180s hit in the league.

Goal: Win the 180s

A simply target, as this will now focus your practice and training and give you a Mantra when playing in the league. Each time you step up to throw in a game, this goal has to be on your mind. **Win the 180s.**

The short-term effect will be to see an improvement in your game scoring. It may be that you even do win the 180s competition.

This first goal has been simple but constructive and has moved you along the route towards county status.

You now sit down and evaluate the next stage. Hopefully you have been recording your weekly practice sessions and we can work from those.

Year two may be to set a target to **regularly average 25+ at Super League**. Again a fairly simple target but here we now need to build a structure around this to ensure it is met.

By this I mean, the weekly practice sessions will need to continue to be focussed, recorded and structured to ensure a continuous improvement.

Remembering our initial goal was to play for the county. Now in year two we are achieving 25+ averages at Super League. It is quite possible that the county management may have already approached you. So what is the next goal to keep your focus and continued progression.

Perhaps time for a step change and let us focus on hitting that elusive **9 dart** 501 game. By now you are competent on hitting 180s. So this season it is about consistency in hitting 7 treble 20s followed up by 81 finish.

How do you remain focussed on these goals

> ➢ No need to tell anyone. They will notice, and what better accolade than for your colleagues to notice your increased 180 count.
>
> ➢ Think about it daily. Find a method to record the fact you are working on this, making sure you just read and see it.
>
> ➢ Build it into your training routine.
>
> ➢ Visualisation. Talking it through in your mind. Perhaps firstly you see yourself hitting 180 after 180. Secondly again in yourself hearing people discussing how you have started hitting a lot of 180s.

You will need to read this chapter many times to ensure you have embraced and absorbed the ideas. Look around and see the professional practising 5 hours a day with the goal of hitting one televised 9 darter each season.

Practise hard, working with achievable goals. The targets will then start to be achieved as you roll through the playing seasons.

As an additional note I mention **flamboyance**. We have discussed a structured training and practice routine with yearly goals built in. We are working toward ultimate goals. We must not forget though to have some fun along the way.

As you improve, perhaps look at something a little different you can build in to your game. Some thing others don't try. It could be absolutely anything. For example you may be on 64 and have three darts in your hand. You go double 14 and double 18. Missing the double would also leave your 50. This is not about belittling your opponent but just having one or two shots in your locker that give you pleasure and are probably only used in light fun games.

**Practice
Routines**

Key Point: *Around 9000 hours of meaningful, planned and measured practice will in most cases result in a highly skilled player. This figure is constant with many other sports.*

So 9000 hours is a figure we will discuss along with where you are now and where you want to be. Also the time you have available and the elapsed period that could be involved.

The first point to consider is the elapsed time factor. If you condense the 9000 hours in to say 6 years. Then with the right conditions etc you may have a chance of breaking into the professional ranks. If 10 hours a week is your total available time, then you may have to revaluate what you can achieve.

The reason for this latter point can be demonstrated thus. An example of a 45-year-old player. Involved in pub darts, Super League and maybe County. S/he has been playing fairly consistently for 25 years.

They may have accumulated 9000 hours, but why are they not hitting 9 dart legs and earning £100k plus a year?

Let us analyse this 25-year profile.

➤ 8 hours per week in some capacity at the oche

➤ Been fairly constant over the 25 years

➤ Good temperament

➤ Reasonable ability

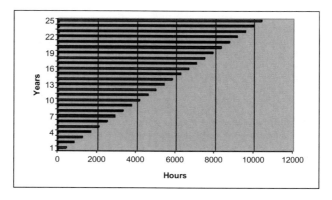

You can see in the above diagram that the 9000 hours is reached in just over 21 years. In most cases as already mentioned it is unlikely that this player has broken through the Super League standard.

The **Key Point** here is the elapsed period.

To reach the professional standard the 9000 hours would be best achieved in a period of about 6 years.

Other factors which may also be affecting our 45 year old player:

➢ Posture and muscle tone

➢ Eyesight

➢ Stamina and fatigue

➢ Motivation and ambition

➢ Lack of structured training sessions

Let us review **Motivation and Ambition**: It cannot escape you that when you are young the world is in front of you, everything is possible. Time is on your side.

There are many examples of older players starting or making the step change and achieving startling results. So from a coaching perspective, there will be different systems to create and work to depending on the starting age and experience factor.

Panacea: A player starting at 14 years of age. Now practising and playing 20 hours per week. In 6 years has accumulated over 6000 hours at the oche. Blending education and darts and now playing youth and possibly County.

Over the next 4 years, another 4000 hours totally just over 10000 hours and just 24 years old. By now physically mature, been playing for 10 years and could be coming out the other side of County, perhaps featuring at national level competitions.

Now we rely on attitude to move this player on. How is this player going to make the transition into say the professional ranks? Perhaps with some elements of the following:

➢ Increase structured training

➢ Financial backing

➢ Mentor to assist with:

    o Competition choice

    o Travelling

    o Sponsorship

Could be in 2 further years, PDC tour card and top 64 in the world and just 26. Seems young, but the player now has 12 years competitive experience. Strong backing and a training and perhaps a business plan to cover the next 5 years.

Above is an ideal scenario with all aspects controlled and delivered. Using the same model we can mould this around many different personal situations. This process could be accelerated, altered and adapted to fit around the circumstances and targets that have been set.

It is worth reviewing the balance between ability, practice and attitude before looking at the practice routines.

In a sport like athletics and in particular the 100-metre sprint, there is no getting away from it that ability plays a key part. Without the correct twitch fibres you are not going to become world champion.

In darts there is far more emphasis on attitude and practice as shown in the following diagrams:

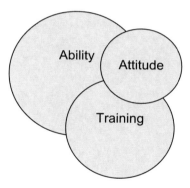

Diagram (1) Athletics

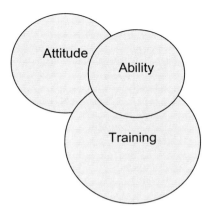

Diagram (2) Darts

Routines:

Note: The following routines are hard work and can seem repetitive. The fundamental idea is conditioning. If you find that you need to mix it up, then there is not a problem with adding or substituting a few alternative games. It may be you decide to play against the computer.

DR1:

This routine DR1 is designed for new entrants to the game and for players who want to improve on their existing performance.

There are 100s of different practice games and ideas already in existence. The idea of DR1 though is to base the schedule on a structured and measured basis. Over time it can of course be amended to suit personal preferences.

The elapsed program runs for 6 months and will require approximately 10 hours per week. At the end of this period you can review your progress and assess the next stage and requirements.

The routine is also based upon you playing in two league games per week. If this is not the case then we can substitute further practice sessions.

Day	Session	Time
1	**Doubles Warm up** *This session is to warm your mind up. So include the Infamous 10 plus 5 or 6 others that you need to work on. This part of the session can be performed at home before going out or at the venue prior to a game.*	30 mins
	Match game	1 hr
2 or 3	**180s only** *Record how many 180s you hit in this session. Keep this figure as part of your training record.*	1 hr 30 mins
4	**Doubles Warm up** *This session is to warm your mind up. So include the Infamous 10 plus 5 or 6 others that you need to work on. This part of the session can be performed at home before going out or at the venue prior to a game.*	30 mins
	Match game	1 hr
5	**Bulls** *Record how many Bulls you hit in this session. Keep this figure as part of your training record.*	1 hr 30 mins
6/7	**Switch** *This will usually be at the weekend. This session is designed to increase your focus and concentration. You start with 20s. The aim is to hit 100 within the three darts. If you achieve this, then immediately switch next throw to a 32 score left. The idea is to check this out without busting it. If you hit the 32 1st or 2nd dart then the go is over. Now switch back to the 20s and so on.* *Record how many Switches you hit in this session. Keep this figure as part of your training record.*	4 hours
	Total training period per week	10 hours

If you only play one game per week replace this session with another 1 hr 30 mins of **Switch**.

Remember you are reading this because you are serious about improving your darts. Now stick to this routine for 6 months and record your results.

There is a sheet at the rear of this manual that can be used to record your progress. At the end of the 6-month period you can analyse your results and improvement in performance. It may be you are ready to embark on routines DR2 or DR3.

You may decide to stay a little longer with this routine and just amend some aspects.

An obvious enhancement for the next 6-month period would be to change the **Switch** target from **32** to **40** and then followed by **36**. This would then see you practising the majority of the common finishing combinations.

DR2:

This is designed for the player who wants to achieve and maintain a 25+ average whether playing in the professional tour or on the amateur circuit.

It will be taken for granted that you have already got personal routines that have helped you attain the level you are now playing at. DR2 though is designed to layer extra structure into your sessions and be adaptable to suit your playing calendar.

We have already seen that to achieve the highest levels of this game we are targeting 9000 hours in a controlled and structured period. This routine will plan to get you there and thereafter maintain this level.

This level of play will need you to be able to have around 35 hours of playing time available.

This will be split between competitive games, structured training and where applicable exhibitions.

Day	Session	Time
1	**180s**	3 hours
	Bulls	2 hours

Record how many 180s and Bulls you hit in this session. Keep this figure as part of your training record.

2	**Switch 140/32**	5 hours

This session is designed to increase your focus and concentration. You start with 20s.

*The aim is to hit 140 within the three darts. If you achieve this, then immediately switch next throw to a **32 score left**. The idea is to check this out without busting it. If you hit the 32 1st or 2nd dart then the go is over. Now switch back to the 20s and so on.*

Record how many Switches you hit in this session. Keep this figure as part of your training record.

3	**Doubles Warm up**	1 hours

This session is to warm your mind up. So include the Infamous 10 plus 5 or 6 others that you need to work on. Keep rotating through this 16 or so numbers.

	Match game / exhibition	4 hours

4	**Switch 140/40**	5 hours

*This session is designed to increase your focus and concentration. You start with 20s. The aim is to hit 140 within the three darts. If you achieve this, then immediately switch next throw to a **40 score left**. The idea is to check this out without busting it. If you hit the 40 1st or 2nd dart then the go is over. Now switch back to the 20s and so on. Record how many Switches you hit in this session. Keep this figure as part of your training record.*

5	**Switch 140/36**	5 hours
	*This session is designed to increase your focus and concentration. You start with 20s. The aim is to hit 140 within the three darts. If you achieve this, then immediately switch next throw to a **36 score left**. The idea is to check this out without busting it. If you hit the 36 1ˢᵗ or 2ⁿᵈ dart then the go is over. Now switch back to the 20s and so on.*	
	Record how many Switches you hit in this session. Keep this figure as part of your training record.	
6	**Doubles Warm up**	1 hours
	This session is to warm your mind up. So include the Infamous 10 plus 5 or 6 others that you need to work on. Keep rotating through this 16 or so numbers.	
	Match game / exhibition	4 hours
7	**Doubles Warm up**	1 hours
	This session is to warm your mind up. So include the Infamous 10 plus 5 or 6 others that you need to work on. Keep rotating through this 16 or so numbers.	
	Match game / exhibition	4 hours
	Total training period per week	**35 hours**

This routine is based upon you playing in three match type environments over the 7-day period. Obviously this may change from week to week and the schedule will need to be adjusted.

There is no problem in building in extra sessions if these match days finish early or indeed do not take place.

Key Point: *It is important to note that it is fundamental that the basic structure is maintained and recorded. Every six months the results can be analysed to assist in assessing whether enhancements are necessary.*

DR3:

This routine is based on upon an evaluation questionnaire formatted around the user's requirements and targets.

For instance as a coach you may be approached by a Superleague player aged 25 and been playing around 5 years. They now want to see if they can step up to the next level at either representative or professional.

Note: an assessment sheet is available at the back of this manual

Following the completion of the evaluation form, you can then work with the subject to design the training programme. (It may be this is a piece of self-analysis).

Two likely approaches:

> ➤ Smooth increase in practice, with focus points on the key elements noted for development.
>
> ➤ Step change

The first option is the less radical. Depending on the focus areas identified, some development will be slower whilst in other areas like maths there may be some quick wins.

With your coach or yourself after completing the DR3 assessment form, sit down and carry out an evaluation process. Let us say you have identified 84 as a problem area when playing out the finish.

Your first dart hits single 20 leaving 64. You now have 2 darts left in your hand. Your opponent is in the finishing straight. You really now have to appreciate that a single 14 is your next shot. Why? So at least you have shot at a double, that being the bull. If after reading this you still go for treble 16, then this manual is not for you, so put it down and lend it to someone else.

Key Point: The whole issue of the above paragraph, is not just being at the oche throwing darts, but continually evaluating options and then building them in to your game.

Using the above detailed method of review and analysis you can continue to work through the assessment form and build the routines that will best assist you to develop your game.

If you have decided to adopt the **Step Change** option, then this is extremely impactive. A point to note is that some of the basic fundamentals may have to be revisited at a later point to ensure they have been mastered.

Firstly an honest appraisal form completed and an assessment what you are now prepared to throw in to the mix. This mix as mentioned includes only a few key areas. DR2 would be used if you wanted to increase performance across all areas in a structured and controlled manner. With **Step Change** perhaps only 2 key areas should be focused on in this three-month period.

The aim here is to make an immediate and dynamic difference to your darting game. So this phase of Step change should be limited to an initial period of three months. When it is finished, carry out a review before decided what the next phase should be.

When the analysis is taking place, we should be looking to for at least a 50% improvement in the areas we wish to see the Step Change take place. So for instance if you practise eight hours per week then this will need to be increased to at least twelve.

Along with the increase in practice it is vital that you build in homework. That is sitting down and analysing all aspects of your game.

Lifestyle

In the professional ranks, money and earning a living are key drivers. There also has to be an acknowledgement that players generally attempt to maintain a healthier life style than perhaps 20 or 30 years ago. That is not to say that many still enjoy a drink and perhaps a curry afterwards. Also as we have discussed in this manual, alcohol does for some have a relaxing effect and even for others as a stimulant.

Alcohol today is about moderation and understanding what your requirements are. For instance, a once a week dart player who enjoys a few drinks with the game seems to fit well into the balanced approach.

Most of this manual concentrates on the player aiming to enhance their game and perhaps looking at County or Professional status. This sort of player is probably playing competitive sessions three or four times a week. With practice sessions this builds up to around 6 times a week at the oche.

To reference the recommended alcohol guidelines, this is something you can do yourself via the Internet, which will then depend on various factors. e.g. male/female, your build and the alcohol content. Suffice to say if you are drinking 6 pints or more throughout these four games, you can already see your weekly consumption is 24 pints plus.

We will use the pints as a nominal drink for ease of explanation. As well as the possible health effects, the cash value per week would be in the vicinity of £70 plus. Which annually would be around £3500 on alcohol alone. Certainly an interesting figure.

So what do we recommend as either a coach or as part of our own self-development.

Firstly there are players now coming through the ranks that do not drink at all and have the temperament to maintain their composure in pressure games without the stimulation from alcohol.

It cannot be forgotten though that for the majority this is still a recreational activity played in pubs and clubs. Also many of these venues sponsor the players, leagues and competitions that we all are involved in.

So how to we build in to our routine factors for health and our budget?

Taking a Superleague player competing three times a week. It may be a simple as saying I can afford £30 per week playing darts as well as the entry fees:

- £30 per week
- 3 games per week
- £10 per night alcohol budget
- Approximately £3 per drink

So in conclusion we need to limit out intake to three drinks to stay in budget. Would this now also assist with achieving the recommend health and alcohol guidelines?

For the unit value on average is 2.3. The recommended government intake is as follows:

- Men 3 – 4 units daily (21 – 28 per week)
- Women 2 – 3 unit s daily (14 – 21 per week)

So with out new regime of a £30 pound budget and 9 pints at 2.3 units, that is equivalent to just under 21 units per week. We can now start to see how we can aim to control our budget and also work towards a healthier lifestyle.

Note: The above paragraphs are purely for awareness and consideration. Exact figures and personal recommendations should be sought from your own health practitioner.

Nutrition: The note above is again relevant to the following paragraphs.

A few aspects to explore with talking about nutrition. As mentioned in the note above, medical and professional advice is always the best avenue for information that is relevant to you.

We can though look at some general principles when approaching the game of darts. We shall discuss energy requirements, health implication and the effects of exercise.

Firstly with energy, this is obtained through many sources from carbohydrates through to fats. What is important is to maintain a consistent source of fuel especially when playing in long and protracted tournaments.

You may see cyclists and long distant runners eating bananas as a quick and easy source of fuel. It is probably better in this manual to work with generalisations and use the DR3 coaching routine to tailor the individual diet and recommendations:

➢ A large meal before practice or a game will use blood to assist with digestion and could make you more lethargic.

➢ Always have breakfast, trying to aim for the healthier option of cereals, toast and fruit.

➢ Try to graze throughout the day especially on these long tournaments. It is no surprise that animals naturally do this. The human seems to be the only species that sits us down, force feeds us three or four courses and tells us off when we do not eat all the food in front of us.

➢ Even with fairly short evening games, it would be sensible to eat light early in the evening and have a healthy snack available during the middle of the evening

➢ Avoid the late curry and chips following the end of play. This will be of no use to you and will cost unnecessary expenditure.

Exercise: We have discussed alcohol used in moderation and a healthy approach to your diet. So what about exercise?

If it were easy, then everyone would be in great shape. It is often hard to start but once you have developed a routine and habit, then keeping going is the best advice.

Note: before starting a fitness campaign, always consult your medical practitioner.

For many it is often about finding something we can fit into our daily lifestyle, hopefully enjoyable, not too expensive and sustainable.

For straightforward weight loss then going for a run cannot be beaten. Swimming and cycling are also good alternatives.

In our early years many of us played sport through our teenage years and some continued through out twenties and perhaps stopping with the added pressure families and work can bring.

So how do we approach this? Firstly get that medical advice so we know what shape we are in and what precautions we need to be aware of. Next it would be useful to understand what we are hoping to achieve.

> ➤ Weight loss

> ➤ General shape up

> ➤ Rehab from illness or injury

Secondly we need to find something that we can hopefully enjoy and is readily available. If you are a professional player on tour, then running will definitely be a suitable option. A pair of trainers and nearly anywhere in the world you are up and going.

Based at home and perhaps a steady club player, then there are many more opportunities. Some will like to train with others, whilst some prefer to exercise alone. For flexibility, sorting your own schedule is simpler but motivation could be a factor.

Whatever you chose, having a final goal in place will help. For instance if you are just starting back after many years and needing to shed a few pounds. Have your medical and perhaps enter a 5k-park fun run in 10 months from now. By entering the date in your calendar as a motivational reminder.

Here are a few general guidelines:

> ➤ Start with a medical and health check-up

> ➤ If for weight loss, keep the target achievable and realistic. Imagine yourself nearly a stone lighter in a year's time. Then all that will be is just over a pound a month in weight loss.

> ➤ Try and enter a low-key event. A short run, charity cycle ride or swim event

> ➤ Three of four session per week

> ➤ Try to take in a gym session once a week. (Note: start with a good induction course/session)

➤ Moderation rather that excess

➤ Find something you enjoy

➤ Remember if it was easy, then we would all look like professional athletes

➤ Keep going, as in a year's time you can look back over the year!!

Smoking: I do not have to say too much here, as there is a huge amount of general publicity around at the moment. Suffice to say it is personal choice and now that you cannot smoke in public places that at least has stopped passive smoking issues at the oche.

You know how much it costs you, and just to remind you with the maths. If a packet of 20 costs on average £5 and you smoke 20 a day, well that is £1,825 per year.

Coaching

This manual can be used in two ways. You may wish to self-coach and appraise your own game. I have made many references to the fact that if you are going to work alone, then an open mind is very necessary.

I would suggest firstly a light read through the whole manual. Perhaps highlighting in the margin areas of note so to come back to at a later point.

Once read through, then you can work on particular areas of interest. To make these sessions efficient, you will need to read and think through what you are trying to achieve. You may disagree or have an alternative method. This will not be incorrect, but at least think through the points made to see if there are any areas when you could adopt for the improvement of your own game

The second scenario is where you may be acting as a coach for a colleague.

To start with you will need the co-operation of the student. Peer advice as seen at the oche works for the odd statement, and perhaps for young players. For instance a kindly word for an inexperienced campaigner about *'leaving it sweet'* when playing pairs may help to develop their game strategy.

To make the coach/student relationship work, co-operation from both parties should be assumed. We shall concentrate on a formal approach in the next few paragraphs.

Stage One: Terms of Reference:

Here both parties agree what the aim of the coaching sessions should be for. What period it should run for. Costs and expenses may be a factor. Location and frequency. All of these are important, so both parties have a framework to structure the coaching sessions.

Stage Two: Assessment:

You may already have a good working knowledge of this player, through being alongside in matches or as a regular spectator. Even so a structured assessment is still necessary.

Hopefully over coffee you will have both agreed the Terms of Reference. Now we can start the assessment phase. There are a few phases to look at. You may choose all of them or conversely pick up the ones that you both have agreed are important to you.

(1). What does the student think? This is an important question. More often than not the player will know what has been an issue with their game. This can be noted down as a starting point. It is not dissimilar to the sportsperson attending the physiotherapist. The first question will most be likely what do you think is wrong and how do you think you did this? A very sensible start to help with the diagnosis.

(2). A couple of light games of 501: This is an early informal look at the player in action. The games will not be of high intensity, but should allow you to observe the player at close quarters. Areas to note will be detailed on the assessment form for DR3 and they are:

➢ Equipment

➢ Speed and rhythm

➢ Stance

➢ Throw and follow through

➢ Body movement

➢ Clothing

➢ Etiquette at the oche

➢ Concentration and focus

➢ Scoring and maths

➢ Finishing

➢ Temperament

(3). Video: This is the final stage of the initial assessment and is a simple as about 10 minutes recording the player at the oche throwing a few practice games. A hand held recorder would be ideal but even the recording from a Smart phone will now suffice. **Note:** Experiment with the best type of shot that will capture your whole body and throw.

Phases 1, 2 and 3 of the assessment stage will allow for the coach to start an early assessment of the player and the coaching targets as agreed at the initial Terms of Reference.

Moving on:

(4). Use the 11-point assessment schedule during a competitive game: Here you agree with the student to be present during some actual games. This has to be approached sensibly in that it should be as informal as possible as not to pressure or embarrass the student. If this could be the case then this phase can be omitted. If though you are assisting a professional player, you may be able to use television footage to assist.

(5). Practice Pads: Allow the student to take these away and build them into their practice and evaluation routines. After warm up we can use the Practice Pads to analyse key target areas in the game. I would suggest we would start with treble 20, double 16, double 20, bull and big 20.

Key Point*: If you have purchased this manual from the CEDL then please use promotional code CEDL001 and your email address to reserve a complimentary pack of 10 pads from* www.centralenglanddarts.co.uk

You should have now completed the assessment stage and are ready to structure the coaching schedule.

As a starting point DR1 and DR2 can be used as template. You then build in the areas where you both agree need additional work.

Key Point*: It is vital that both also agree how you are going to monitor progress and overall achievements. Hopefully you have both agreed a medium term goal and timescale that will give you a firm target point. For instance it may be to start playing Superleague in the next season whilst maintaining a 20 plus dart average.*

Along the route it will be necessary to build in review milestones. Some of these will naturally occur. You as the coach may also be playing in the same league as your student and will be able to monitor their progress. Alongside this also agree regular meetings. I would recommend monthly and this works for most durations of coaching. For example if you have agreed a 9 monthly schedule, then 9 meetings will be factored in.

Key Point*: Part of you role as coach is to continue to identify:*

Is the schedule still relevant?

Is it being kept to?

Is achievement progressive?

Areas that may need to be adapted

Motivation

You will need to assess the student and the schedule achievements continually. Do not be frightened to adapt and change. It is important that you and the student both understand what you are aiming for.

There will be time when it does not seem to be going to plan. This is where you earn your spurs. A reminder perhaps what has already been achieved, a reminder of what you are working towards and perhaps just being there to chat with.

A great statement to encompass all of the above is from golfer, Arnold Palmer:

"It's a funny thing, the more I practise the luckier I get"

Key Point: *Please remember all of the above where we refer to a coach, or it could be working by yourself . You will need though to be disciplined and still work and adopt the same practices as outlined above.*

Scoring

This is a short chapter dedicated to those who struggle with either counting as they play or when with pen in hand at the side of the board as match scorer.

We won't look at the professional circuit but concentrate on developing techniques to help in both of the scenarios as mentioned above.

Some players have a great mathematical brain and they often struggle to understand why so many have trouble with the numbers. There may be a few reasons, ranging from perhaps being number blind, nerves, lack of practice or just needing a leg up to understand the best methods.

There are some players who knowing they struggle a little with the actual maths, learn the majority of the combinations by rote. In this manual we hope to development an understanding of the numbers and some coping methods to get you under way.

On the Chalk Board:

Today many venues have electronic score boards. You still need to know the actual score to key in to the machine. Some players will assist by calling their score as they approach to retrieve their darts.

Others will be quiet and expect you to do the counting. In most sanction competitions, the electronic score board may be replaced by chalk or dry wipe boards. So to start with we will concentrate on adding up the three darts thrown and then we will look at the subtraction.

Key point: concentrate on adding up the darts thrown and do not try to pre-empt by counting down to a finish. Certain to get in a pickle by attempting this.

Firstly adopt a standing position at the chalk board that covers the following points:

> ➤ Far enough back so you can see the darts thrown
> ➤ Do not move during the throw
> ➤ Perhaps slightly aside to allow the audience to see the score board

I would suggest from the offset you add the darts up as they hit the board. Two reasons for this. Firstly you may be asked by the player to assist with confirming what they have left and secondly it will help you build up to the final score.

For some this is not easy process. There is no issue with adopting a controlled approach when adding them up and then saying the score aloud and asking the player to confirm. This way you and the player are in agreement with the score that will be used to subtract from the running total.

Key Point: *always write the agreed score on the board prior to the subtraction.*

501		501	
100	401	60	441
75	326	140	301
57	269		

Diagram (3)

If you do get the score wrong or later the subtraction, at least the two players and you can see the historic progression of the game.

Ok we now come to the subtraction. There are many ways people do this, but I will explain one method for you to start with. As you progress and get more confident you may develop short cuts and other quicker ways.

Key Point: *Right to Left always.*

So how does this work in practice? Let us take the board at diagram (3). The player is on 326 and their next three darts are 20, 20 and 17 giving a total score of 57.

Firstly confirm the score with the player, and then write the 57 on the board.

Now in your mind place the 57 under the 326:

$$\begin{array}{r} 326 \\ \underline{57} \\ 269 \end{array}$$

Figure (4)

As in the key point, start from the right. Attempt to take 7 from the 6 above. It will not go, so borrow a ten unit and take 7 from 16 leaving 9.

Then as you have borrowed a ten unit, you now change in your mind the 5 to a 6 and attempt to take it from the 2. It will not go, so borrow a ten unit and take 6 from 12 leaving 6.

Then as you have borrowed a ten unit take 1 from the 3 leaving 2. And the final answer is 269.

Now just keep practising this method at home with all types of combinations and it will work for you in the game.

Tips on you scoring your darts during the throw:

It is important as your game improves that you know your way around the board.

As demonstrated in the chapter on finishes, if you are sitting on 228 a score of 60 will not be of much use as it will leave you 168 and no three dart finish. Would it have not been better for you to have been aware of this trap and gone perhaps 20, 20 and 18 leaving 170 your favourite three dart finish?

So straightaway you will notice you need to start thinking about what you have in front of you on the score board and what you can throw to best leave your self a winning opportunity.

This will be assisted if you can develop a process in your mind to assist with counting what you have thrown and what you have left.

To start with it is look at what you have before you throw and what is needed to leave a finish. In most cases when you are in the 200s for example a treble 20 is the first dart of choice. The tip now is to know what the minimum score is to leave you that three dart finish.

This will help. As if you are accurate with your throw, as the last darts goes in you will be left on a finish. This also has a secondary benefit of perhaps letting your opponent know that you are comfortable around the board.

If what ever reason a couple of darts have not hit their intended target, then we need to readjust to attempt to leave that elusive three dart finish.

There is absolutely no issue with conferring with the scorer if you have one. You may confirm what you have scored and what you have left. (Beware though their maths may not be as good as yours).

Two darts thrown. Stop and take stock of where you are. Once you become more proficient this will become a seamless adjustment. At this stage though, if you are not sure of your finish, take your time and get it right.

**Key
Points
&
Sayings**

Key Point: You will need to warm up both mind and body. ....

Key Point: If after two darts you have left your finish with an odd number. Concentrate on your last dart to leave the score as sensible as possible. No wasted darts. This is all part of the conditioning and will prevent you from throwing wasted darts during a game. ....

Key Point: Be Mr/Mrs Cool. Eliminate from now any signs of emotion. Keep the heart rate under control. Approach the throw in a controlled and consistent manner. Do not swear. ....

Key Point: It may help to develop a mantra. By this I mean when you practise at home you have a saying/picture/theme in your mind as you focus on the game. This is used for instance in golf and snooker when approaching a match winning put or shot. ....

Key Point: Keep the pulse rate under control. ....

Key Point: During the practise sessions it is important that you develop this high level of concentration. ....

Key Point: From now on we will focus on you having the ability to take on the big finishes and that by the time you have worked through this manual and practised, your darts' maths brain will also be vastly improved. ..

Key Point: The Infamous 10 finishes: ....

Key Point: The mental side of your game is now important. After changing your darts, any loss of form or a bad shot has to be either accepted as the bedding in period for the darts, or even that the dart change has not contributed to this. It would extremely counter productive to revert back to your old set-up without a full consolidation period of at least 6 months using this new configuration. ....

Key Point: Around 9000 hours of meaningful, planned and measured practice will in most cases result in a highly skilled player. This figure is constant with many other sports. ....

The **Key Point** here is the elapsed period...

To reach the professional standard the 9000 hours would be best achieved in a period of about 6 years..

Key Point: It is important to note that it is fundamental that the basic structure is maintained and recorded. Every six months the results can be analysed to assist in assessing whether enhancements are necessary..............

Key Point: The whole issue of the above paragraph, is not just being at the oche throwing darts, but continually evaluating options and then building them in to your game. ....

Key Point: If you have purchased this manual from the CEDL then please use promotional code CEDL001 and your email address to reserve a complimentary pack of 10 pads from www.centralenglanddarts.co.uk ....

Key Point: It is vital that both also agree how you are going to monitor progress and overall achievements. Hopefully you have both agreed a medium term goal and timescale that will give you a firm target point. For instance it may be to start playing Superleague in the next season whilst maintaining a 20 plus dart average. ....

Key Point: Part of you role as coach is to continue to identify: ....

Is the schedule still relevant? ....

Is it being kept to? ....

Is achievement progressive? ....

Areas that may need to be adapted ....

Motivation..

"It's a funny thing, the more I practice the luckier I get" ....

Key Point: Please remember all of the above where we refer to a coach, or it could be working by yourself . You will need though to be disciplined and still work and adopt the same practices as outlined above. ....

Key point: concentrate on adding up the darts thrown and do not try to pre-empt by counting down to a finish. Certain to get in a pickle by attempting this. ....

Key Point: always write the agreed score on the board prior to the subtraction..

Key Point: Right to Left always. ....

There are 100s of sayings that accompany the game. We will feature a few here, which seem to take place when you are at the oche.

Often these sayings derive from a blend of common sense and proven techniques. A little like Old Wives' Tales, today these are validated by science and current analyses. So let's explore a few:

Go on like you do:

> Not sure I approve of this. It is designed to help motivate you and remind you of your ability. It will be shouted by your colleagues as an attempt to get you going. I think I would think I am trying and do not need this sort of perceived motivation. May work for some though.

Have it out, you left it:

> Quite jovial, a gentle reminder that probably you have a split a very sensible finish to something a little more difficult. For example you have been on 40 and you hit double one leaving 38.

Got three darts so use them:

> Often said when you have hit the winning double with your third dart.

Pick it up:

> Another attempt at motivating by your mates. It would be useful if you are the sort of player that occasionally loses concentration or focus.

I am a rhythm player:

> This refers to comment made by yourself for yourself. It should remind you to concentrate and keep a steady pace to your throw.

Usually one follows the other:

> We all know that when you are throwing well it all seems so simple and the second and third darts just arrive at the same point as the first. This is good if the first dart was thrown accurately. You may see some players taking longer with their first dart ensuring it hits the target, then just letting the next two just flowing in to the same area.

Head on:

> We have talked about temperament and here this refers to you stopping the antics that may be disturbing your composure at the oche.

Let's have a look:

> Quite a good saying. It reminds us that it is very important to prepare before throwing the first dart. This approach ensures you look at the target before throwing. How often do you notice that when you aim at the middle of the target double, you actually hit it. So why when we are throwing for score, you don't look at a specific treble target.

Just let them go:

A reference to relaxing throughout the shot.

Give us a shot:

When playing a gentle game of pairs, this is hoping the opposition miss their out shot.

Big and black, the rest will come:

Some time during the game, you may be trying to force the score and not being able to get going. Here you are reminded that start again with hitting 3 big twenties. Then it is quite interesting when the last dart often dips into the treble twenty giving you a score of 100.

I practise the stuff I cannot hit:

When training time is perhaps short or you are in the phase before a match or a competition. Concentrate on those areas where you are a little weak. Obviously you need to ensure you are comfortable with three darts in the twenties. But what about the 75 that sometimes eludes you?

It is for you to deal with when you are at the oche:

Simply when you are facing a problem during a match, you need to understand it is up you only to sort it out. Try not to come away from the oche after a match blaming the slow play of your opponent or the temperature etc. Find a way during the game to overcome the mental issue and concentrate on winning the game.

Look at what you are aiming and aim at what you are looking at:

If you have actually looked at the target, then make sure you continue to throw the dart at this initial target.

3 in the big bed:

Similar to as mentioned before, concentrate on hitting three twenties.

Have a good look at it:

As you approach the oche, this comment is designed to remind you to concentrate on the target especially on a game shot. Already it can be seen how many of these sayings accentuate the vital point of focus and concentration.

Big and red:

Not sure if this actually helps. This is a reference to aiming at the treble twenty. It is usually commented on when you are attempting to hit the 100 plus score shots and it is not quite happening.

One out One in:

The next two sayings mean the same and really are quite sensible: The whole ultimate endeavour is to have feeling and control over the throw. It is not always possible to be absolutely exact with the first dart. So it is so much better to have the first dart sitting in a non-scoring area just outside the double. By now you should have developed a feeling and a small variation should give you an opportunity to hit the target.

One over one under:

As above.

Don't go for a single where the treble could bust you:

We all make this mistake at some point. When in an important game, condition yourself to aim at numbers that won't bust your score. For example you have 54 left, I know it can be tempting to throw at a single 18 especially with the safety option of 4 just below. But occasionally you will hit the treble 18 and lose the option at a shot to win the game.

Relax:

A gentle reminder to keep that all important composure at the oche.

Straight down the tube:

A pleasant saying to assist with your visualization. Imagine you need double 10 to win the game. What better thought than your arm, hand and throw travel down an imaginary tube all the way from you to the target.

Record sheets

DR1:

Sheet:

Week/Commence	180s	
	Bulls	
	Switches	
Week/Commence	180s	
	Bulls	
	Switches	
Week/Commence	180s	
	Bulls	
	Switches	
Week/Commence	180s	
	Bulls	
	Switches	
Week/Commence	180s	
	Bulls	
	Switches	
Week/Commence	180s	
	Bulls	
	Switches	
Week/Commence	180s	
	Bulls	
	Switches	
Week/Commence	180s	
	Bulls	
	Switches	
Week/Commence	180s	
	Bulls	
	Switches	
Week/Commence	180s	
	Bulls	
	Switches	

DR2:

Sheet:

Week/Commence	180s	
	Bulls	
	Switch140/32	
	Switch140/40	
	Switch140/36	
Week/Commence	180s	
	Bulls	
	Switch140/32	
	Switch140/40	
	Switch140/36	
Week/Commence	180s	
	Bulls	
	Switch140/32	
	Switch140/40	
	Switch140/36	
Week/Commence	180s	
	Bulls	
	Switch140/32	
	Switch140/40	
	Switch140/36	
Week/Commence	180s	
	Bulls	
	Switch140/32	
	Switch140/40	
	Switch140/36	
Week/Commence	180s	
	Bulls	
	Switch140/32	
	Switch140/40	
	Switch140/36	
Week/Commence	180s	
	Bulls	
	Switch140/32	
	Switch140/40	
	Switch140/36	

DR3:

Name:	
Age:	
Gender:	
Years playing:	
Standard:	➤ Pub average 15+ ➤ Superleague average 20+ ➤ County average 22+ ➤ Representative average 25+ ➤ Professional average 30+
Weekly routine:	
Weekly practice hours:	
Last 2 years honours:	
Weekly games:	

	DR3 continued
Perceived weaknesses by the player.	➤ Equipment ➤ Speed and rhythms ➤ Stance ➤ Throw and follow through ➤ Body movement ➤ Clothing ➤ Etiquette at the oche ➤ Concentration and focus ➤ Scoring and maths ➤ Finishing ➤ Temperament
Observations by the coach:	➤ Equipment ➤ Speed and rhythms ➤ Stance ➤ Throw and follow through ➤ Body Movement ➤ Clothing ➤ Etiquette at the oche ➤ Concentration and focus ➤ Scoring and maths ➤ Finishing ➤ Temperament